# 1960s

John Abberley

THOSE who lived through the decade will always call it the Swinging Sixties. It was the time when Harold Wilson invented the permissive society and girls wore mini-skirts and dashing young men drove a Mini Minor. President Kennedy was assassinated and just before the end of the 1960s two Americans became the first men on the moon. In Britain, there was almost as much excitement in 1966 when England won the World Cup.

In North Staffordshire it was an era of demolition and reclamation. Fine old buildings like Newcastle's Municipal Hall came crashing down, while huge yellow earth-movers pushed Berry Hill pit mound into a nearby marlhole. City council leader Sir Albert Bennett described the scheme as "putting hills into holes".

At the outset of reclamation Stoke-on-Trent had 2,600 acres of derelict land. The bottle ovens had been snuffed out, but hundreds still dotted the skyline. After the celebration in 1960 of the golden jubilee of the Federation of the Six Towns, the succeeding decade was an ideal time to improve the drab Potteries scenery.

It was also a time of change in the pottery industry. Buyouts became the order of the day and famous names like Shelley were swallowed up by bigger operators. Bob Cant, elected as MP for Stoke Central in 1966, urged a policy of diversification in local industry, warning that "the pots and pits won't last for ever".

Berry Hill Colliery was the first of 12 North Staffordshire pits to close in the 1960s, although millions of pounds were invested in modernising deep mines like Hem Heath and Silverdale. Thousands of men arrived from the North East to work in the mines and many families from Durham and Northumberland settled on the Bentilee estate, introducing a fresh element in the area's social life.

The 1960s saw the end of an era on the railways with the disappearance of steam trains. Hanley, Burslem and Tunstall lost their stations with the closure of the Potteries Loop Line, as did Newcastle on the route to Market Drayton. On the other hand, the journey time to London was drastically cut by the new electric trains. The opening of the M6 motorway in 1963 also brought great benefits to the area in terms of travel and transport.

In 1962 the Victoria Theatre set up shop in a converted cinema at Hartshill and a sparkling epoch began for the company specialising in theatre-in-the-round. Director Peter Cheeseman created a kind of theatre new to the area, the historical documentary with songs.

Meanwhile, Hanley's rebuilt Theatre Royal had gone over to bingo, so the nearby Gaumont Cinema doubled up as a venue for live entertainment as well. Famous groups like the Beatles and the Rolling Stones appeared on stage there and big shows were presented by amateur societies. The Queen's Hall, Burslem, was also brought into use for live theatre.

However, the early 1960s saw the closure of old-established cinemas like the Essoldo, Hanley, and the Hippodrome, Stoke.

In 1962 a night club called The Place opened in an old warehouse in Bryan Street, Hanley, instigating a sea-change in the area's night life. The Golden Torch ballroom opened at Tunstall and the Penny Farthing Club in Hanley. People travelled from Liverpool and Manchester for a night out in the Potteries.

Finally, the local sporting world of the 1960s was dominated by Stanley Matthews, who returned to Stoke City at 46 and took them to promotion before retiring at 50 when he became the first footballer to be knighted.

Many of these personalities and events are reflected in around 200 photographs, although this book cannot be regarded as a comprehensive review of the decade. As in the previous Sentinel publications, most of the pictures are taken from the paper's own archives. For other contributions my grateful thanks go to the Potteries Museum, Jim Morgan, Peter Cheeseman, Lonnie Cook, Peter Johnson, Phil Bradbeer, Ann Gredington, Dave Scragg and David Rayner.

# The Way We Were
## in the 1960s

# Contents

4     Out & About

36     Family Entertainment

74     Clubs & Pubs

94     Sport

124     Transport & Emergency Services

# Out & About

Anyone born soon after the Second World War will remember
the drab North Staffordshire scene. By the end of the 1960s it
was looking better. Overall, the area was a much cleaner place,
thanks to smoke control and grassy patches on previously derelict
sites. But scores of old buildings went under the bulldozer. The
centre of Hanley briefly looked like a bomb site and the city
lost historic relics like the Hill Pottery at Burslem, along with
hundreds of the area's traditional bottle ovens. At Newcastle, the
imposing Municipal Hall was demolished in spite of strong public
protests, as was the Castle Hotel apart from its Georgian frontage.
However, the opening of the M6 motorway in 1963 brought
welcome relief for Newcastle town centre, which had been choked
for years by passing traffic on the A34 trunk road.

Helicopters were rarely, if ever, seen flying over built-up areas when this formation zoomed less than 100 feet above Newcastle Guildhall in 1968. The machines, from the RAF Central Flying School at Tern Hill in Shropshire, were taking part in a flypast over North Staffordshire to celebrate the RAF's 50th anniversary. The old wartime station at Tern Hill had friendly links with Newcastle. When the RAF finally left, the base near Market Drayton became an army barracks.

There was a touch of class about Henry White's shop, which stood on the site of the Roebuck coaching inn in Newcastle High Street. Sutherland House, seen here in 1967, sold clothing for women and children. Henry White's other shop in the Ironmarket specialised in men's wear. Sutherland House was opened in 1887 and closed around 1980, along with the Ironmarket premises. The Georgian buildings in High Street have been replaced by the Roebuck Centre.

Up to the mid-1960s, noise and fumes from nose-to-nose traffic on the A34 trunk road was part of daily life in Newcastle. The only route for drivers was straight through the town's traditional shopping centre, with heavy lorries thundering along the narrow High Street only a couple of feet from market stalls. This 1960 picture shows a typical scene in High Street, as seen from a corner of Lancaster Buildings.

Museum curator Paul Bemrose met the seafaring hero Admiral Nelson head to head in 1968 after a bust of the great man was removed from its lofty perch on the old Borough Treasurer's Office at Newcastle. The four-foot effigy was made as a tribute to Nelson after his death at Trafalgar in 1805 and had been fixed to the office in Nelson Place for 150 years. It was renovated and repainted before being put on permanent display at Newcastle Museum.

When this workman removed part of the foundation stone of Newcastle's Municipal Hall in 1967, he found a sealed glass bottle containing documents placed there at the time of the stone-laying in 1888. However, those who left the time capsule would have been surprised to learn of its discovery after less than 80 years. The borough council's controversial decision to demolish the imposing Municipal Hall was bitterly opposed by many townspeople.

Newcastle Mayor Denis Proctor catching up with all the news of 1888 after opening a time capsule discovered during the demolition of the Municipal Hall in 1967. The newspaper was one of a number of items placed in the sealed bottle. With the mayor in his parlour are the mayoress, Mrs Proctor, Newcastle's Town Clerk C J Morton, deputy borough surveyor Eric Stock and museum curator Paul Bemrose.

Newcastle had its own version of a space rocket in 1964 when this realistic model formed part of Newcastle 'lights' in Queen's Gardens. Originally conceived as a miniature version of Blackpool's autumn illuminations, the annual event came up with a topical theme as its centrepiece. After being dropped for a while, the lights have returned in the form of a Christmas feature.

This Newcastle butcher added Christmas trees to his Christmas offerings in 1969. According to a Sentinel report, there were plenty of turkeys that year, but game birds were in short supply and selling at around 8s (40p) a brace. A gift box of Black Magic chocolate cost 11s (55p). And in 1969 there were no hygiene laws to prevent the butcher from hanging up his festive birds outside the shop.

Rain made the pavements glisten and even the Sentinel seller had temporarily left his post when this picture was taken at Newcastle in December 1960. Christmas shoppers were out with their umbrellas looking for bargains on the market stalls. At that time traffic was permitted on both sides of the market. Newcastle's first market charter was granted in 1173.

A view looking down Newcastle Ironmarket in 1965 when it was still a busy traffic route in both directions. On the right demolition work was taking place on old properties and the dominant Municipal Hall on the left was to follow 12 months later. The bus on the left belonged to the Princess Bus Service, which ran between Newcastle and Silverdale.

This large hole appeared at the southern end of Newcastle High Street in 1964, signalling the start of work on the sunken Grosvenor roundabout. The old properties on the left were demolished up the Black Friar pub. In the distance is the white frontage of the Castle Hotel, then still in business.

A rear view of what had once been the Castle Hotel, Newcastle's old coaching house and the town's premier social rendezvous. The building dated back to the early 1800s. After the bulldozers did their work in 1969, the only part left standing was the three-storey Georgian facade, which was preserved after the intervention of Newcastle Civic Society. The site was occupied for a short time by a Tesco store, but has since been put to other commercial uses.

Bill Webber, pictured in 1967 when he became the top man in North Staffordshire scouting after taking over from the legendary Marshall Amor as secretary of Stoke-on-Trent and Newcastle Divisional Scout Council. He remained in the job for 25 years and in 1984 was awarded the scout movement's highest honour, the silver wolf. For many years Bill was chorus master of the long-running local scout show, Screamline. He was born in London and came to this area as a wartime Bevin Boy to work underground in the pits.

A council workman gathers autumn leaves and other waste on the sunlit public gardens at Boothen known as the Boulevard, laid out along the bed of the old Newcastle Canal. The year was 1964 and the area's flora was well established on the reclaimed land. The canal started as an offshoot of the Trent and Mersey and and went underneath the centre of Stoke before following a route to Newcastle.

Snapshot of Longton from the air on a surprisingly bright winter's day on January 1, 1962. The main Uttoxeter Road cuts through the middle of the picture, with the bottle ovens of the Gladstone Pottery (then Thomas Poole and Gladstone China) almost in the dead centre. Other clearly visible landmarks include the Empire Cinema on the extreme left in Commerce Street, Aynsley's factories on the right in Sutherland Road and Longton market and town hall in the top left-hand corner. Patches of empty land show that clearance of derelict potbanks had already begun.

A rooftop view across Longton town centre in 1965 from the tower of St John's Church, which was soon to be demolished. Behind the twin domes of Longton town hall is the half-built Bennett Precinct with its modernistic clock tower. Longton's newly-completed bus station is in the middle background.

This steeplejack had a superb view across Longton from his perch on top of the 213-foot Harvey's Chimney before it was demolished in 1962. The chimney was actually in the grounds of Thomas Forrester's pottery works, but was built in the 19th century by a man named Harvey, a local banker. It was believed to be the tallest chimney in the pottery industry and only second in height to the mighty stack at Chatterley Whitfield Colliery, Tunstall.

Burslem appeared to be on the verge of a new era in 1960 with the opening of a town centre garden and bandstand funded by the Civic Trust. It was seen as the first step in a long-term plan to reinvigorate the Mother Town. The garden, built on the site of the old meat market and Norris's wine merchants, comprised two tiers of terracing, a bandstand, raised lawn area, toilets and public seating covered by a canopy. Small memorials to the novelist Arnold Bennett and local war hero Jack Baskeyfield VC were added later. However, the whole area has since been flattened to make way for the Ceramica project.

The Hill Pottery was such a dominant feature of the Burslem landscape in Arnold Bennett's day that the author used it as the model for his 'Sytch Pottery' in the novel Clayhanger. Indeed, it was called "the wonder of Burslem" when Samuel Alcock opened the works in 1839. The imposing building with a Venetian-style entrance changed hands many times before it eventually fell into dereliction and was demolished in 1966. The site was believed to be associated with the earliest potting in Burslem in the 16th century.

Apart from the cars and the Co-op Store in Swan Square, Burslem town centre in the early 1960s was little changed from that in Arnold Bennett's day. The building in the centre of the picture is the George Hotel and on the right is the original Swan Bank Methodist Church, later to be demolished. At that time the Mother Town still had plenty of bottle ovens and chimneys, several of them smoking. The photograph was taken from the top of the Royal Doulton factory in Nile Street.

A piece of Arnold Bennett's Burslem disappeared in 1960 with the demolition of Norris's wine merchants and the meat market, which shared a large 19th-century building alongside Burslem's old town hall. James Norris bottled a range of wines, spirits and beers including the popular Highland Queen whisky under his own label. In post-war years the company sold rum at 18s (90p) a bottle. The meat market had a distinctive frontage with classical Greek columns.

A tranquil scene at Cobridge Park in 1962, with the oval-shaped bowling green as its central feature. In the background are the huge bulk of the Sneyd Colliery pit mound and the headgear of the colliery itself. The railway signal box on the left is near Cobridge Station on the Potteries Loop Line. In 1962 the railway still had a passenger service, though it was discontinued a year later. On the right is the famous Moorcroft Pottery, which then had its complement of bottle ovens.

This was the last picture to be taken of the village institute at Trentham, standing beside the A34 when the trunk road was still a single carriageway. It was built by the Duke of Sutherland in 1894 to provide a recreation centre for local people. The institute, along with other beautiful properties, was demolished in 1960.

With the coking plants of Shelton Steelworks forming the backcloth, young spectators at a cricket match practise their own skills on the boundary. The year was 1960 when the works at Etruria had a cricket field on an area called the Old Hall Pond. The pond had been filled in, largely by rubbish from the Wedgwood factory. At that time Shelton Bar was of the John Summers group, but was later renationalised under British Steel.

Another view of the 1960 national boat rally on the canal at Stoke, with the high wall of the British Rail goods depot rising from the water's edge on the right. The scene on this short section of the Trent and Mersey Canal remained unchanged for a century until the building of the A500. The huge gasometer at Etruria is in the distance.

Two prominent landmarks hold the key to finding your way around this panoramic view across Stoke in 1967, the dome on the Co-op Emporium on the right and the square bulk of the College of Ceramics in the midde distance. In the centre of the picture is the rear side of the old Salvation Army hostel in Lovatt Street. On the horizon behind the college are the chimneys and wooden cooling towers of the former Hanley electricity works.

Even with traffic flowing in both directions, the scene in Glebe Street, Stoke, had a leisurely air on this summer's day in 1960. The flag was flying on Stoke Parish Church of St Peter ad Vincula, probably in celebration of the golden jubilee of Federation of the six towns. Up the street opposite the church entrance is St Peter's Chambers, then still standing alongside Stoke town hall. The passing PMT bus masks a spot where there used to be a Victorian drinking fountain.

Skyscraper flats were something new in Stoke-on-Trent when this model of an urban renewal scheme in Hanley was made in 1964. Potteries people were used to living in small houses at ground level and mining subsidence was another factor against building upwards. However, the scheme at Bucknall New Road was up and running before the end of the 1960s, incorporating 11-storey blocks of flats. Viewing the model were the city council's housing chairman Jim Westwood and George Mellor, of the city architect's department.

A civic inspection of work in progress on one of Stoke-on-Trent's reclamation schemes to remove old pit mounds at Fenton. Huge earth movers cleared many derelict industrial sites, which were replaced by large patches of attractive grassland. With Lord Mayor Mary Bourne are council leader Sir Albert Bennett, Councillor Ken Wright, Town Clerk Keith Robinson and Councillor Alf Ellerton.

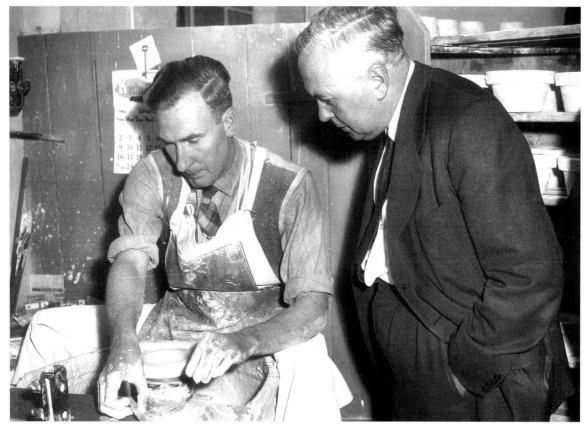

During a brief visit to the Potteries in 1962, Harold Wilson was taken to the old Minton factory in Stoke, where he chatted with pottery thrower Ted Wood. Mr Wilson was then chairman of the Labour Party and Shadow Chancellor. Two years later he was Prime Minister.

Although Harold Wilson wasn't even leader of the Labour Party in 1962, he was still an honoured guest of Stoke-on-Trent Labour Party. Mr Wilson, then Shadow Chancellor, is seen at Stoke town hall receiving a teaset from Les Sillitoe, who at that time was president of the National Society of Pottery Workers. In the centre is Harriet Slater, MP for Stoke North for 13 years and a Labour whip after Mr Wilson became Prime Minister in 1964.

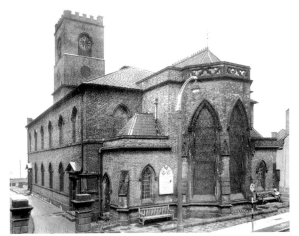

Regular services were being held in Stoke-on-Trent's oldest Anglican church, St John's in Hanley, when this picture was taken in 1962. In more recent times, the 18th-century listed building has been surrounded by controversy following efforts by the Lichfield Diocese to sell off the property, which has been empty since 1986. This move has been strongly resisted by a campaign group, the Friends of St John's Trust, who want to turn the redundant church into a Christian drop-in centre. Prince Charles has expressed his support for a restoration scheme.

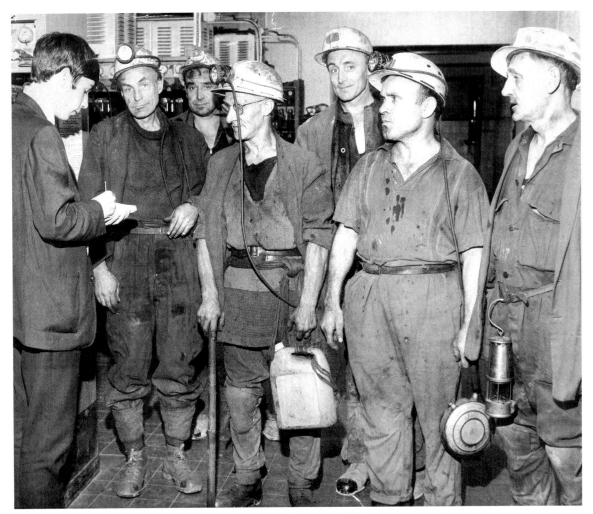

Sentinel reporter Peter Colbeck, left, seeking the views of miners at Wolstanton Colliery in 1968 about proposals to move the Potters' Fortnight annual holiday. It was later switched from the traditional first two weeks in August to June/July. After the sinking of a new shaft in 1961, Wolstanton Colliery became Britain's deepest coalmine at that time. It was closed in 1985.

This was Sneyd Colliery, one of 12 North Staffordshire pits which closed in the 1960s due to the ever-decreasing demand for coal in both homes and industry. In the foreground is the conveyor which took colliery waste to the top of the huge tip. On January 1, 1942, Sneyd was the scene of the area's last major pit disaster. An underground explosion killed 57 men and boys. Normally, the colliery would have been deserted in accordance with a superstition about working on New Year's Day, but the miners went down in answer to an appeal from the wartime Government.

These miners might have managed a smile, but they had just finished their final shift at Parkhouse Colliery and were going their separate ways. The pit was closed in 1968 because of difficult wet conditions on the coalface after almost a century of coal and ironstone mining. The cage which brought the men back to the surface after the last shift was powered by a steam-driven winding engine which went back to Parkhouse's beginnings. Even so, the small colliery beside the A34 road at Chesterton had a weekly output of around 7,000 tons. At the closure it employed more than 450 men. Nowadays, the site is occupied by an industrial estate.

A busy scene in Campbell Place, Stoke, in the 1960s, with the bottle ovens of the Spode Copeland factory emerging above the rooftops. It was a time when traffic passed through the town centre in both directions, unhindered by a one-way system. The Wheat Sheaf Hotel on the right had its original frontage, but the Grapes pub had disappeared from the cleared site marked with the notice Sold.

It used to be called Tunstall Market Square, but under Stoke-on-Trent's street renaming scheme it became Tower Square in tribute to the yellowbrick clock tower dominating the top end. This was erected in 1893 on the site of Tunstall's old town hall when the market square was still used for its traditional purpose. The Sneyd Arms on the right was rebuilt in a modern style around 1945. The picture was taken on a wintry day in 1960.

Labour's Leader of the Opposition, Hugh Gaitskell, renewed his ties with the Potteries in May 1960 at the official opening of Burnwood County Secondary School, Chell Heath. He reminded the large audience of his involvement with the WEA movement in Stoke-on-Trent. Also on the platform were two city, Mrs Harriet Slater and Dr Barnett Stross. Mr Gaitskell, on a two-day visit, addressed a United Nations rally of 1,400 people at the Queens Hall, Burslem. However, the man who would have been Labour's next Prime Minister died suddenly three years later.

Prime Minister Harold Wilson, wearing his trademark raincoat and carrying his famous pipe, waves to supporters on arriving at the Victoria Hall, Hanley, to address a 2,000-strong rally in 1967. Outside the hall he was greeted by anti-war demonstrators urging him to support an end to America's war in Vietnam. But when Mr Wilson walked onto the platform he was given a standing ovation before speaking on national affairs for 75 minutes. At that time the only other Prime Minister to have visited Stoke-on-Trent was Ramsay MacDonald in 1931.

"Come up and see us sometime" thousands of shoppers did just that to see what was on offer in the cockloft at the old Hanley General Market. They climbed the stairs to a noisy gallery where there were all kinds of livestock for sale, including dogs, cats, cage birds, rabbits, ferrets, hens and day-old chicks costing one old penny apiece. The site of the 19th-century market building is now occupied by the Potteries shopping centre.

Charles Street Wesleyan Methodist Chapel, once a bastion of Hanley's religious life, is seen here in the final stages of demolition in October 1961. Its origins stretched back to the 18th century and John Wesley himself, who preached at a small chapel close to the site in 1784. The much larger building was opened in 1819 and attracted congregations of up to 500. The chapel was still in use in the late 1950s.

This spectacular view from the top of one of Hanley's tallest chimneys illustrates that even in the late 1960s bottle ovens were still a prominent feature of the landscape. It was the last chance to capture this scene as the chimney at Ashworth's pottery was demolished soon afterwards. With Broad Street running down the centre, the photograph shows scores of old properties which vanished to make way for the Potteries Way ring road. In the bottom corner on the right is one end of the building which then housed Old Betty Plant's sweet factory.

When bulldozers demolished the old Hanley General Market in 1981 they also removed Derricott's fish and chip shop, which had its roots in the 19th century. The Derricott family took over the business in Town Road (then High Street) in 1922, though it had already been a fish and chip shop for many years. In more recent times the shop and cafe were busy all day, with queues stretching down the street. The picture was taken in the 1960s.

A ban on cigarette advertising was far into the future in 1965 when an illuminated Woodbines sign shone out across Crown Bank, Hanley. The hoarding high up on the corner of Piccadilly and Stafford Street has long disappeared and the buildings in the right background have been replaced by a modern shopping complex. The toilet block in the centre of the picture has since been rebuilt.

For a couple of decades the Minister at Bethesda Methodist Church, Hanley, acted as chaplain to the staff at Lewis's store. His weekly duties included holding a short service on the second floor before the store opened. In this 1962 picture farewell gifts are being presented to the Minister, the Rev J Brazier Green, on his departure from the area. On the right are Mr W G Doughty, head of Lewis's in Hanley, and Mr George Miller, general manager.

Look carefully at this picture and you can pick out demolition workers standing precariously near the top of the tower of the Hanley Trinity Presbyterian Church. On this occasion in 1966, however, the 19th-century church was not about to be demolished but being given a more modern appearance. One historical titbit: the earliest local company of the Boys' Brigade was established there in the 1890s.

Ten Potteries girls had the ride of their lives when a parade of circus elephants wound its way from Stoke to Hanley in 1965. They were chosen from 50 girls who answered an appeal by Billy Smart's Circus for volunteers to ride on the animals from Stoke Station to the circus site off Harding Road, Hanley. Among them was 17-year-old Gill Forrester, pictured here on her elephant. At one point she almost fell off when it stopped to pick flowers on a roundabout.

End of the show at the Essoldo Cinema, Hanley, in the summer of 1962 when the huge building in Stafford Street was demolished. Previously known as the Palace, it became a cinema in 1932 after a varied history as a roller skating rink, ballroom and boxing venue. The world boxing champion Primo Carnera fought an exhibition bout there shortly before the changeover to a cinema. The Essoldo was reputed to have the largest CinemaScope screen in the Midlands.

In the 1960s era of wholesale demolition, Hanley town centre sometimes resembled a bomb site. This is the end of the Marquis of Granby, a popular Victorian pub in Crown Bank on the corner of Market Lane. The large building in the background is the old Stoke-on-Trent Telephone Manager's Office.

When this picture was taken in Hanley Market Square in 1966, the end was near for the historic home of Henry Pidduck and Sons, the long-established jewellers next door to the National Provincial Bank. The notice at the entrance told customers that the shop had moved to temporary premises after 125 years on the site. Following the completion of new premises, Pidducks returned to their traditional place until the business passed to new owners. The old shop was used to display the Blue Riband of the Atlantic, a trophy presented by the Hanley MP Harold K Hales.

Horse meat in Hanley? Yes, it was once sold at these derelict premises in Broad Street. A notice at the City Horse Meat Shop advised customers that the meat was for dogs and not for human consumption. The eyesore property was demolished in 1964, along with others in the row, under a city council road-widening scheme.

When minor improvement work was carried out in Hanley Market Square in 1968, the scene had changed little since the 19th century, apart from the modernised frontage to the Angel Hotel. For many years the pub was a favourite eating house for Hanley businessmen. Next door is the Grapes pub (also known as Wilders) and a corner of Hanley General Market is visible on the left.

A rainy day in Lamb Street, Hanley, in 1968 when cars could travel up the one-way street into Market Square. On the left is the newly-finished Hanley Island which replaced a large block of mixed properties, including the old Lewis's store and the original Pidduck's jewellery shop. Huntbach's store on the right had been given smart new frontages, but the old-established family business later closed down.

# Family Entertainment

For theatre lovers in North Staffordshire, one door closed and another opened in the 1960s. Only 10 years after it was rebuilt and reopened in 1951, Hanley's Theatre Royal went over to bingo. But this loss was offset in 1962 by the opening of the Victoria Theatre at Hartshill as a permanent home for theatre in the round. Amateur musicals found new homes at the Gaumont Cinema, Hanley, and the Queen's Hall, Burslem. The Gaumont stage became a regular setting for star visitors like the Rolling Stones. The ABC Cinebowl, a combined cinema and bowling alley, was added to Hanley's attractions. Longton's new bus station also incorporated a bowling alley on the upper floor. However, both these bowling ventures were short-lived. In 1968 a new element was added to North Staffordshire's family entertainment with the opening of BBC Radio Stoke-on-Trent in studios at Cheapside, Hanley.

The sign says the Gaumont, but to several generations of Burslem people this old cinema was the Coliseum or "the Col" for short. Before it was converted into a cinema in the 1920s, the Coliseum was a popular variety theatre and music hall. The Potteries-born star Gertie Gitana sang there in 1917. It had its own orchestra and later a Compton cinema organ was installed. Although the Col was in the same street as another cinema, the Palace, both drew the crowds in the 1940s. The name was changed to the Gaumont in the 1950s, which proved to be the final decade. The cinema closed in November, 1960, when this picture was taken.

Stoke-on-Trent's long-running scout show Screamline returned to the Queen's Hall, Burslem, in 1964, after the city's main theatre in Hanley went over to bingo. Although the Queen's had to be converted from a dance hall into a temporary theatre, the production still played to full houses. Screamline originally made its debut at the Queen's in 1934, modelled on Ralph Reader's famous gang show. The picture shows a scene from the 1966 show at Burslem, with scouts dressed as dancing troupe girls at a carnival.

In the harsh winter of 1963, there were many playtime tumbles at this school in Milton, where the playground was turned into a skating rink by the hard frost. The harsh weather lasted for two months in what was recorded as the coldest winter for a century. Rivers and even the sea in the English Channel were frozen. The football programme was wiped out for weeks in what The Sentinel called 'The New Ice Age'.

This graphic painting by Terence Cuneo captures the defiance of Lance-Sergeant Jack Baskeyfield, who won a posthumous VC at Arnhem in 1944. The courage of the young soldier from Burslem inspired a 90-minute film made by amateur cine enthusiast Bill Townley. It was completed in 1969 and shown as part of ceremonies held at Burslem to mark the 25th anniversary of Baskeyfield's heroic stand against advancing German tanks. He was Stoke-on-Trent's only winner of the Victoria Cross in the Second World War.

In 1967 the New York musical West Side Story was thought to be too difficult for amateurs to stage because of its demands on dancers. But under the direction of ex-ballet dancer Willie Martin, the North Staffs Amateur Operatic Society proved the doubters wrong with a dazzling show at the Queen's Theatre, Burslem. The fighting between the rival gangs, the Sharks and the Jets, was so realistic that blood was spilled and one dancer was concussed. The picture shows the Sharks during an outdoor rehearsal.

Ramblers and a party of scouts pause for refreshments at Wetton Mill during a November hike in the Manifold Valley in 1964. A beautiful section of the valley near this spot was preserved for walkers and cyclists when plans to convert the track past Thor's Cave into a road for motor traffic were dropped. Until 1934, a narrow gauge light railway ran through the Manifold and Hamps valleys from Waterhouses to Hulme End.

A bowling alley on top of a bus station? This novel combination was introduced by the owners of the PMT Bus Company at Longton in 1964 at the opening of a new bus station for the town. But the idea didn't catch on with the public and the alleys were later dismantled before being replaced by Jollees night club.

Summertime in the early 1960s at a place called Bucknall Sands, where children paddled and bathed safely in the shallow waters of the River Trent. Several generations of youngsters enjoyed outdoor swimming at this favourite spot close to the Leek road at Abbey Hulton. A similar setting on a brook running through nearby Bentilee was also known as Bucknall Sands.

Would you believe it? In 1965 this sturdy poplar tree grew out a rough stake which was supporting the sapling being held by a Sentinel reporter. In fact, a whole row of 20-foot-high poplars grew from stakes, dwarfing their small partners planted along the frontage of a Midlands Electricity Board sub-station in Locketts Lane, Longton. A city parks official said it was an unusual occurrence, but not unknown in the horticultural world.

After previous problems when staging big shows at Hanley's Gaumont Theatre, Newcastle Amateur Operatic Society came of age with Oklahoma! in 1969. With a string of hits like O What a Beautful Morning and Out of My Dreams, the production was a great success. Although the cast included Newcastle stalwarts like Don and June Collings, the society borrowed a number of experienced guest performers to take principal roles. In this scene Curly (Alan Hulme) is wooing hard-to-get Laurey (Shirley Woods). In all, Alan has played Curly five times with different societies.

These fathers gave boys of the 2nd Cheadle Scouts a helping hand with the cooking on a wood fire at Kibblestone Camp, near Stone, in 1965. However, cooking breakfast was a real hit-or-miss business 20 years earlier because the previous generation of campers were allowed only two matches to light a wood fire. Kibblestone was first used by scouts in 1927 after the land was made available at a nominal rent by the potter Ronald Copeland. It later developed into an international camp site visited by scouts from all parts of the world.

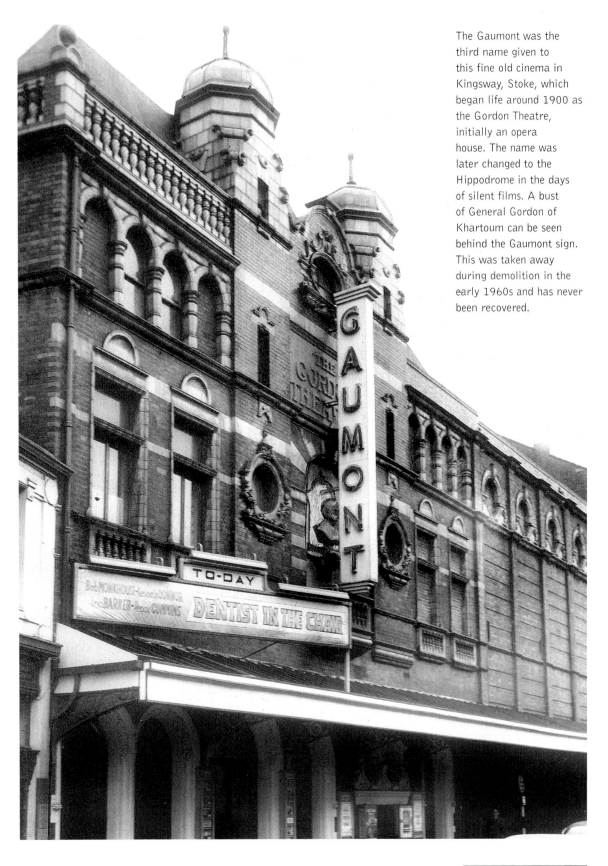

The Gaumont was the third name given to this fine old cinema in Kingsway, Stoke, which began life around 1900 as the Gordon Theatre, initially an opera house. The name was later changed to the Hippodrome in the days of silent films. A bust of General Gordon of Khartoum can be seen behind the Gaumont sign. This was taken away during demolition in the early 1960s and has never been recovered.

To mark the centenary of Arnold Bennett's birth in 1967, another literary giant, J B Priestley, delivered a lecture on the Five Towns novelist which was broadcast live on the BBC Third Programme. It was staged before a packed audience in the Jubilee Hall, Stoke, as part of a weekend of Bennett celebrations. Priestley is in the centre of the picture with Lord Mayor Ted Holloway and two former first citizens, Jim Evans and Horace Barks. Behind them are Keele's Professor Roy Shaw, who later became Director-General of the Arts Council, and Town Clerk Keith Robinson.

This face was familiar to hundreds of people who dined at the North Stafford Hotel in Stoke up to the end of the 1960s. It belonged to the hotel's long-serving head waiter, Clarence Turgel, known to patrons only by his surname. Born in France, Turgel was renowned for his decisive manner. He remained a fluent French speaker in spite of spending most of his life in this country.

Visitors had the company of this family of resident swans during the National
Boat Rally in 1960. The craft included converted narrow boats, ex-working boats
and estuary cruisers. An historic steam boat arrived from Cheshire. A prize was
awarded for the boat which had travelled the longest distance and another for the
most hazardous journey. An army colonel came to the rally from Berlin and a couple
travelled from the Persian Gulf.

There was hardly a
mooring space for a
mile along the Trent and
Mersey Canal when the
National Boat Rally came
to Stoke in 1960. A total
of 147 craft crowded
into the stretch of canal
between Liverpool Road
and Whieldon Road and
the rally attracted 30,000
visitors over five days.
Lord Mayor Gordon Dale
is seen waving from a
boat after performing the
opening ceremony. The
event was organised by
Stoke-on-Trent Boat Club
as part of the city's golden
jubilee celebrations.

What happened to this bust of General Gordon which looked down from the old the Hippodrome Cinema in Stoke for 60 years? It was last seen being put on a lorry after the building was demolished in 1962. Originally called the Gordon Theatre, it was briefly an opera house and variety theatre before becoming a cinema around 1920. The name was changed to the Gaumont in the 1950s.

Thanks to the insistence of a young curate, a pancake race was established as an annual event in the village of Werrington. The curate, Patrick Ashton, persuaded a dozen female parishioners to take part in the race along Washerwall Lane. The only rule he made was that the contestants had to toss the pancake at least three times while on the run. Mr Ashton is seen about to start a race in the early 1960s.

In spite of being situated in the centre of the city, the first headquarters of Stoke-on-Trent Boat Club was literally in a quiet backwater just off the Trent and Mersey Canal in Stoke. The club, housed in a disused corn store alongside the old Newcastle branch canal off Copeland Street, initially had about 130 members. Many owned boats converted from craft like lifeboats and pontoons. In 1960, only three years after its formation, the club played a host to a national boat rally. The picture was taken by Jim Morgan in 1968 before the clubhouse was demolished to make way for the construction of the A500 road through Stoke.

The entire cast of the musical Carousel, presented in 1965 by the newly-formed
Newcastle Amateur Operatic Society at the old Municipal Hall, Newcastle. The show's
success encouraged the newcomers to stage their second production at the Gaumont in
Hanley. Carousel was the last show at the Municipal Hall before it was demolished.

A pile of rubble covers the site of the former Roxy Cinema after the demolition of
the 19th-century building in Nelson Place, Newcastle, in 1963. It began life as the
Newcastle and Pottery Theatre and in 1910 took the title of Cinema Theatre when the
first silent films were shown. In 1930 a new owner changed the name to the Plaza
and in 1946 it became the Roxy, closing in 1957. Queen Victoria's statue stood in this
location for many years before being moved away.

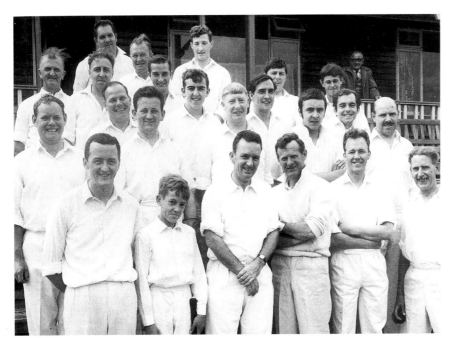

Besides trying to outdo each other on the musical stage, the North Staffs and Stoke-on-Trent operatic societies were also friendly rivals on the cricket field. The teams are seen before a match at Newcastle and Hartshill Cricket Club in 1967. The two captains, Alan Collier and Frank Edwards, are in the centre. Inevitably, there were hearty sing-songs in the bar after the matches.

Strong social links have been built up between the adjoining villages of Ipstones and Foxt, near Cheadle, through a senior citizens' association formed 50 years ago. When this group of country folk was set up in 1953 as an old age pensioners' association, members were charged 1s (5p) a year. Activities included summer mystery trips and Christmas parties. A large party of members are pictured in 1960 after an evening trip to Stone.

Stardom on the London stage was still a long way in the future for Gordon Alcock when he played Captain Corcoran in HMS Pinafore at Cheadle in 1965. It was his final role with Cheadle Choral Society after appearing in half-a-dozen Gilbert and Sullivan productions at the Carlos Institute during his seven years with the group. Gordon is in the centre in a scene with Arthur Gilbert (Sir Joseph Porter) and his son David (Midshipman). After turning professional Gordon was in his 50s before he finally reached the West End stage, playing the lead in A Passionate Woman opposite Stephanie Cole when he was 59.

Although it hasn't broken box office records, The Merry Widow has probably been staged more times than any other show in North Staffordshire. So when Stoke-on-Trent Amateur Operatic Society presented this much-loved musical at the Theatre Royal, Hanley, in 1960, the cast knew they had to rise to the occasion. The title role of Anna was played by Mary Wilkinson, a concert singer making her debut in a musical romance. In this scene the Can-Can girls are seen strutting their stuff at Maxim's.

Even when the best films were showing, audiences at the former Regent Cinema in Hanley welcomed a break for live music played on the Wurlitzer organ. The white-painted instrument, which rose vertically out of the orchestra pit, was played by many famous organists over a period of 40 years. A local perfomer at the keyboard was Trevor Tildsley, seen here in 1960 entertaining children at the Saturday Club. He was sometimes hit by popcorn and crisps.

One of the first eight stations in the BBC's local radio network went on the air on March 14, 1968, from studios in Cheapside, Hanley. BBC Radio Stoke-on-Trent was launched thanks to an annual grant of £52,000 from the city council for the first two years of broadcasting. At the outset the programmes went out on VHF only and the number of listeners was limited. The picture shows members of the original team of broadcasters with the station's first manager, Harold Williams, second from left. The others (left to right) are Owen Bentley, John Abberley, Mike Stephens, Arfon Roberts, David Gredington, Susie Hillman and John Cordeaux.

Hanley greyhound track at the old Sun Street Stadium was among the pioneers when it opened in 1928, staging meetings on three nights a week. For many years money usually changed hands in shillings and sixpences, although an occasional punter would place a bet of £100. Greyhound racing never attracted more than 200-300 people, but local bookmakers like Alec Moss, Tom Donoway and Alf Davies often had a hectic time. It remained in business until the stadium closed in the 1960s. The picture shows part of the floodlit track.

Hospital radio, known as North Staffs Broadcasts to Hospitals, was controlled by David Gredington in the 1960s until he left in 1967 to join the team which launched BBC Radio Stoke. In the picture he is seen receiving a farewell gift from a hospital radio colleague, Irene Fisher. On the right is David's wife, Ann, also a hospital broadcaster. On the left is Tom Wilson, who was chairman of a long-running quiz on hospital radio, and at the back is John Broun, whose programmes included A Seat in the Circle about films showing at a local cinema. The hospital broadcasting service has now closed down after 49 years.

A splashing time was had by all in Hanley Park's paddling pool, which was a great attraction when it opened in the 1960s as an adjunct to the nearby playground. On hot days children from a wide area cooled down in the pool and sunbathed on the surrounding grassy banks. Unfortunately, it fell into disuse and the area was filled in.

This was the larger of the two pools at Hanley Baths, where several generations of Potteries children learned to swim. The Victorian building also housed Turkish and private baths, which were much in use in the days when few families had a house with a bathroom. The baths was formerly the home of swimming champion Norman Wainwright, who represented Britain three times at the Olympic Games. The building was demolished in the 1960s.

Queues outside the old Odeon Cinema in Hanley to see Alfred Hitchcock's thriller Psycho, showing in 1960. The 1,300-seater Odeon, built on the site of the Grand Theatre, was the last word in cinema luxury when it opened in 1937. In the late 1940s the Odeon employed Ivor Jones, who at 3ft 11in was reputed to be the smallest cinema page boy in Britain. In the 1960s The Sound of Music ran for 12 months. But the Rank Organisation closed the Odeon in 1975 and the building was later converted for use as a wine bar.

Shoppers in their hundreds braved the rain to welcome Santa Claus on his arrival in Hanley in the late 1960s. The coach was followed by a parade of floats and pantomime characters, usually starting from Tunstall. Santa later entered Lewis's Store down a specially-constructed 'chimney'. Picture courtesy of Vince Heath.

Tenpin bowling came to Hanley in 1963 with the opening of the Cinebowl, a large new building also housing a cinema, seen here in the final stages of construction. It was the country's first purpose-built cinema and bowling alley under one roof. However, bowling finished in 1973 and the basement alley was converted into the Heavy Steam Machine discotheque and later became Churchill's casino. The cinema closed in the 1990s.

No-one in the audience ever saw him, but as back stage manager Hughie Dix played an important part in the success of any show at the Theatre Royal, Hanley. Hughie is in the centre of this picture, surrounded by dancing girls of the North Staffs Operatic Society before a performance of Annie Get Your Gun in 1960. Also in the picture is Hughie's tiny dog, Mitzi.

On a warm summer day Trentham Baths was like a magnet to Potteries people. At its peak, the outdoor pool beside the lake in Trentham Gardens attracted as many as 10,000 visitors in a single day. With its art deco buildings and woodland surroundings, the pool enclosure resembled the set for a Hollywood film. It remained a favourite playground for 40 years until subsidence damage forced its closure in 1975. The whole area was later bulldozed.

There was room for everybody on the spacious dance floor at Trentham Gardens
Ballroom, pictured here in the 1960s when it was still the premier rendezvous of the
Potteries. In the big band era Joe Loss and his Orchestra played there half-a-dozen
times a year. It later became a venue for top cabaret entertainers and pop groups.
Picture courtesy of Philip Bradbeer, former general manager.

How did they explain this to the children? In the early 1960s Santa Claus spent part of his journey on board a pleasure boat on the lake at Trentham Gardens, accompanied by festive maidens. He then travelled to Lewis's in Hanley in a more traditional manner by horse-drawn coach. Picture courtesy of Dennis Harrison.

Swimmers brave the ice-cold open-air pool at Freshwater, near Leek, in the early 1960s. The popular summer venue on the Macclesfield road between Rudyard and Rushton was opened in the 1930s by a local businessman who also organised open-air dancing on the dam at Rudyard Lake. He produced a postcard for the swimming pool advising people to "get away from the smoke-laden towns and enjoy the pure sparking country air of Freshwater". After it closed around 1970 the pool was converted into a trout farm.

Can you recognise this fresh-faced young man standing outside the old Victoria Theatre at Hartshill in November 1962? It's the renowned playwright Sir Alan Ayckbourn, then an actor and budding writer with the Vic's first resident company. He was about to write a children's play called Christmas Versus Mastermind, which was performed at the newly-opened theatre-in-the-round, along with his other early works. A couple of years later Ayckbourn moved to the Vic's sister theatre in Scarborough and in 1970 became its artistic director. He is now regarded as Britain's greatest living comedy playwright.

A good view of the Victoria Theatre's auditorium at Hartshill, taken during a rehearsal for A Christmas Carol in December 1965. At that time the converted cinema had a capacity of 350, later increased to around 400.

When The Jolly Potters was staged at the Victoria Theatre in 1964, it introduced audiences at Hartshill to plays based on local history. In this case the action was concentrated on the part played by pottery workers in the Chartist Riots of the 1840s. Joseph Capper (Bernard Gallagher) is seen addressing a mass meeting of strikers at Crown Bank, Hanley, supported by the Chartist Thomas Cooper (Stanley Page). It was the first of a series of musical documentaries directed by Peter Cheeseman which helped to establish the Vic's reputation.

In reflecting developments in the 19th-century pottery industry, The Jolly Potters included this scene called the cup-making machine. In the foreground Gordon Reid and Wanda Moore make a point as a cup flies in mid-air between them. In one or two performances the cup was dropped. The play ran for four weeks.

This scene in The Jolly Potters was called the Battle of Burslem, illustrating an episode in 1842 in which a man was shot dead when soldiers fired on the rioters. The central figure is actor Gordon Reid, who is appealing to a group of fellow Chartists, while a magistrate stands opposite with a blindfolded prisoner. The scene shows how theatre in the round works with minimal scenery and stage props.

The Staffordshire Rebels, the Victoria Theatre's 1965 documentary, enlightened many people about Staffordshire's close involvement in the 17th-century civil war between King and Parliament. There was a skirmish betweeen Roundheads and Cavaliers at Hopton Heath outside Stafford and a man from Newcastle signed the death warrant of Charles I. This scene represented a re-enactment of the Battle of Marston Moor in Yorkshire in 1644, a turning-point in the war.

Two Vic actors who achieved international fame, Robert Powell and Ben Kingsley, are seen in this opening dance sequence from The Staffordshire Rebels with Fiona Walker and Amelia Taylor, daughter of the historian A J P Taylor. After leaving Hartshill Powell played the title roll in the film Jesus of Nazareth, while Ben Kingsley was knighted following a string of stage and screen successes.

This was how the Victoria Theatre presented the trial of Charles I at Westminster Hall. Tony Handy (right) played the King, Ron Daviels (centre) was General Thomas Harrison and Robert Powell was Judge John Bradshaw. Newcastle-born General Harrison was second-in-command to Oliver Cromwell and Bradshaw was Newcastle's Recorder.

Ben Kingsley in the part of the miller who nearly captured the disguised Charles II, the king who supposedly hid in an oak tree at Boscobel on the Shropshire border to frustrate his pursuers.

One of the most successful productions to be staged at the Victoria Theatre was The Knotty, a musical documentary about the North Staffordshire Railway, which was known as the Knotty because of its Stafford Knot emblem. It was first staged in 1966 and finally topped 200 performances. The script was created by Peter Cheeseman and resident playwright Peter Terson, working with a team of old railwaymen. Cheeseman (left) and Terson posed before the first night on the 'Knotty cloth' depicting the railway network.

A snapshot from the pole dance sequence in The Knotty, representing the myriad of plans for lines by different railway companies before the birth of the North Staffordshire Railway in 1846. The dancers depicted rival surveyors who appeared to use their poles as weapons.

A retired railwayman, Harry Sherratt (second left), comes face to face in a rehearsal with Christopher Martin, the actor who played him. Harry was one of a number of ex-Knotty men who helped to create the play's authentic dialogue. Alongside him is director Peter Cheeseman and on the left is another Vic actor of that era, Edward Clayton.

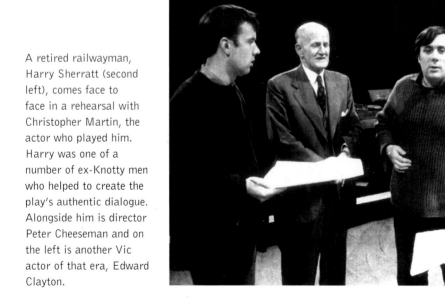

A crafty lawyer from Nantwich (Brian Young, centre) clinches a cheap deal for Oak Farm, the land on which the Crewe railway junction was later built. The simple farming couple were played by Susan Tracey and Christopher Martin.

Holding his walking-stick, the Knotty's legendary general manager, W D Phillips (Brian Young), is the pivotal figure in this scene during the railway strike in 1919. Four years later the North Staffordshire Railway came to the end of its independent existence on amalgamation with the LMS Railway.

# Clubs & Pubs

Night clubs were practically unknown in North Staffordshire
until the arrival of The Place in Hanley in 1962. Its phenomenal
success was followed by a proliferation of new night spots like
the Penny Farthing, Hanley, the Golden Torch Ballroom, Tunstall,
and the Cameo, Longton. Rock bands replaced dance orchestras
at traditional venues like the King's Hall, Stoke, and the Queen's
Hall, Burslem. The "beat boom" created by the Beatles produced
many talented local bands. Indeed, in the 1960s there were more
bands on the road in the Potteries than in any other decade. They
were playing somewhere in the district every night of the week
and a few had records in the national charts.

Fans crowd around the stage as teenage pop singer Lulu performs at the King's Hall, Stoke, in the 1960s. Lulu sang one of her first major hits, a rock 'n' roll number called Shout. The King's Hall was a regular venue for up-and-coming stars, with as many as four groups following each other on stage. On one Saturday night in 1962 it cost only 10s (50p) to see the Beatles, Gerry and the Pacemakers, The Big Three and Billy J Kramer and the Dakotas.

Another view of Legendary Lonnie Cook in performance with Carl Mann before an audience of admiring fans at the King's Hall, Stoke. One of Lonnie's most popular numbers in the 1960s was Wine Glass Rock, in which he ran a wine glass up and down the strings of his guitar. He appeared at almost every live music venue in the area and has never given up performing. He still does gigs at the age of 61.

Carl Mann singing at the microphone with Legendary Lonnie Cook backing on lead guitar at the King's Hall, Stoke, in 1964. At the time Lonnie performed with Carl Mann and the Candymen before setting up his own group. The King's Hall was a favourite venue for beat groups. It wasn't unusual for at least four different ones to appear on stage on the same evening.

There was a wild welcome for Tom Jones when the Welsh singer gave a performance at the King's Hall, Stoke, in 1965. Jones the Voice, as he was then called, was already on the way to international stardom. He sang his first hit "It's Not Unusual". Jones also came to the Gaumont, Hanley, in 1968.

In tune with the Swinging Sixties, Bry Martin and the Marauders were pictured sitting on a swing in Hanley Park. The group from Brown Edge reached the national pop charts with their single That's What I Want. Left to right are Danny Davis, Kenny Sherratt, Bry Martin and Barry Sargeant.

Joint owner Bill Morris looking over plans for extensions to The Place in 1968, by which time membership had grown into tens of thousands. The famous club in Bryan Street is still operating after more than 40 years.

Stoke-on-Trent's night life entered a new era in 1962 when The Place night club opened in an old warehouse in Bryan Street, Hanley. Booking top groups of the day, the club established a reputation which attracted visitors from a 50-mile radius. The picture was taken in 1968 when the joint managing directors, Bill Morris and Kevin Donovan, announced plans for extensions.

As soon as its doors opened in 1966, the Penny Farthing discotheque in Charles Street, Hanley, was a hit with the sophisticated smart set. Stoke City footballer Eddie Stuart perfomred the official opening, riding in on a penny farthing bicycle. These customers being served with drinks were typical of the clientele.

Former policeman Mike Massey, who was first employed as a doorman when The Place opened in the 1960s. Loyal and hardworking, he rose to the position of managing director of Jollees night club at Longton and worked closely with stars like Cliff Richard, Cilla Black, Andy Williams, Danny La Rue and Tommy Steele.

As always, the dance floor was crowded at the Penny Farthing in Hanley, a small nightspot with an intimate atmosphere. It attracted girls in mini-skirts and chiffon scarves with bobbed haircuts and men in sharp suits. In 1974, this successful addition to the city's night life was sold to The Place entertainment group.

Bill Morris, left, and business partner Kevin Donovan, the entrepreneurs from Manchester who launched The Place night spot in Hanley in 1962. It grew into an empire which included The Placemate at Newcastle and Jollees night club, Longton. These enterprises were divided when the pair later split up.

This was how the Queen's Hall, Burslem, looked in 1966 before improvements were carried out to make the stage suitable for large-scale musical productions. At that time it was still a venue for Saturday night dances. A raked auditorium was installed and the name was changed to the Queen's Theatre. It provided an alternative venue for amateur shows when Hanley's Theatre Royal was no longer available.

When it came to playing New Orleans traditional jazz, nobody in the Potteries did it better than the Ceramic City Stompers, seen here in full flow. Formed in 1954, they played their earliest gigs in Burslem at the old Embassy Club and the Moorland Road Cafe. On one occasion they played at the Cavern in Liverpool, sharing the evening with the Beatles, who then called themselves the Quarrymen. In the early 1960s the group moved to the Crown and Anchor Hotel, Longton, and stayed together until venue closed around 1964. In the picture the players (left to right) are Arthur Wood (bass), Bob Williams (clarinet), Dave Timmis (drums), Mel Hill (trumpet), Joe Stephenson (banjo) and Phil Rhodes (trombone).

Tunstall acquired a new reputation for its night life with the opening of the Golden Torch ballroom in 1965. It was the brain-child of Chris Burton and Keith Fisher, trading as the Chris Wainwright Agency, who converted the former Regent Cinema into a dance venue which became widely known as a centre of Northern Soul music. A feature of the ballroom was its abstract murals on a Roman theme. The premises in Hose Street were later destroyed in a fire.

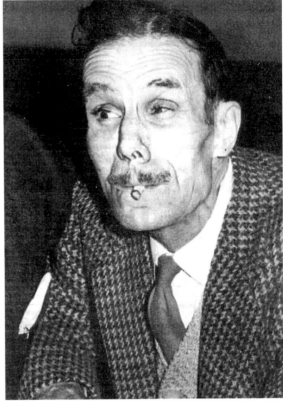

Potteries stand-up comedian Jack Simms, whose non-stop wit was enjoyed by thousands of people in the workingmen's clubs of North Staffordshire. At his peak in the 1960s, Jack could keep an audience laughing for 45 minutes without a break. Among his repertoire of comic songs, The Sheik of Araby was a great favourite. Ill-health eventually forced Jack's retirement as a part-time entertainer.

A pair of cast-iron balustrades adorned the frontage of one of Newcastle's oldest pubs, the Hind's Vaults on the corner of High Street and Lad Lane, seen here in 1967. The distinctive ironwork was probably added in Victorian times, along with a barrel sign above the front entrance bearing the date 1843. However, the timber-framed property was built in the 17th-century. The pub and adjoining premises were demolished to make way for a row of modern shops.

American rock star Little Richard entertaining fans in a packed crowd at Trentham Gardens Ballroom in the 1960s. The extrovert performer, remembered for a string of hits like Baby She's Got It, is seen on stage with entertainments manager Les Johnson standing immediately behind. Picture courtesy of Peter Johnson.

While he was leader of the resident band at Trentham Gardens Ballroom, Reg Bassett rarely played before a crowd of less than 1,000 dancers. Yet the popular orchestra was run purely as a hobby by the bandleader, who admitted that he was never taught to read music. Over a period of 20 years, he employed a succession of talented performers, including the vocalist/songwriter Jackie Trent. Reg Bassett is seen fronting the band in the early 1960s.

Whether it was upstairs in the Highland Room or downstairs in the main ballroom, Ray Piper and his Music were popular performers at Trentham Gardens. The five-piece group was formed in 1965 when Trentham's director of entertainment, the famous bandleader Geraldo, wanted a band for dinner-dances in the Highland Room. However, they still appeared in the ballroom at weekends supporting Reg Bassett. In the picture Ray Piper is on the extreme left playing the organ.

The big band sound still retained its popularity in the 1960s, particularly when Ted Heath and his Orchestra were the visitors to Trentham Gardens. In this picture by former Sentinel picture editor Huston Spratt, dancers crowded in front of the stage to welcome the bandleader. Seated by the piano are singers Denis Loris, Lita Rosa and Dickie Valentine.

The Fab Four took the stage at Trentham Gardens in 1963 before a capacity crowd of 3,000 fans. At that time the Beatles were already a household name. Entertainments Manager Les Johnson said afterwards he could have sold enough tickets to fill Stoke City football ground. However, there was a big disappointment for the crowd. Their heroes played for only about half-an-hour and didn't return for a second spot.

# Sport

Any award for Potteries sportsman of the sixties would surely have gone to Sir Stanley Matthews, who returned to Stoke City when he was 46 and took the club back into the top flight before hanging up his boots. Stoke also celebrated the club's centenary in 1963 with a memorable game against Real Madrid. For Port Vale the 1960s are best remembered for FA cup exploits rather than for the blot on their record when they were briefly expelled from the Football League in 1968 for illegal payments. In cricket, top-class internationals like Gary Sobers and Jim Laker played for clubs in the newly-formed North Staffordshire and South Cheshire League. In snooker, former Hanley policeman Ray Reardon made his mark as a top player after turning professional. But speedway came to an end at the Hanley Stadium in 1963 three years after it was revived.

One of Britain's tennis stars of the 1960s was Keith Wooldridge, from Longton, who was among the top six men and a member of the Davis Cup squad. In 1966, he reached the third round of the men's singles at Wimbledon and faced the American Stan Smith on the Centre Court before a 16,000 crowd. Wooldridge gave a good account of himself, but lost in straight sets. As a junior, he played at Wimbledon against his great rival, Stan Matthews junior. Wooldridge was formerly a member of Stone Lawn Tennis Club.

Former top tennis player Jeremy Bates inherited his aptitude for the game from his father Sam, seen standing in front of the net (with hand on hip) at Bucknall Park in 1968. Sam, a keen doubles player with Tunstall Park, was taking part in a men's tournament, along with wellknown sportsman and Lord Mayor Doug Brown, seen on the left. Jeremy Bates, who won the Wimbledon mixed doubles title with Jo Durie in 1988, was born in the Potteries but moved to Birmingham as a child.

The mighty South African tourists were in no mood to ease up against the Minor Counties at Longton in 1960, winning the two-day match by nine wickets. Former England Test player John Ikin, who captained the Minor Counties team, is seen near the centre of the picture wearing a dark blazer. Fourth from the right is the future England wicketkeeper Bob Taylor, who was then Ikin's teammate at Bignall End. The match marked Taylor's debut in first-class cricket. The Springbok's captain, Jackie McGlew, is on the extreme right of the players in striped blazers.

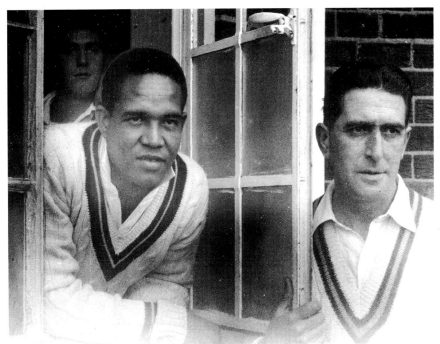

Gary Sobers, the greatest all-rounder of his day, watching a match at Norton in 1964 through the dressing-room window, with Norton captain Jim Flannery on the right. Sobers was the club's professional for two seasons at a time when big names dominated the North Staffs and South Cheshire Cricket League. Sobers was later knighted, as was a previous Norton professional, Sir Frank Worrell. Away from cricket, Jim Flannery was a useful goalkeeper who played for Stoke City Reserves.

An exhibition cricket match at Burslem's old ground at Cobridge in 1960 was made memorable by one huge six-hit by the England star Basil D'Oliviera. The ball landed on the civic Rolls-Royce and left a dent in the mudguard. However, Lord Mayor Gordon Dale was still happy to shake hands with D'Oliviera and the rest of the players who took part in an event to mark Stoke-on-Trent's golden jubilee. Those in the picture include West Indians Wes Hall, Roy Gilchrist and Sonny Ramadhin, Australians Cecil Pepper and Jack Pettiford, Burslem's president Tom Donoway and Staffordshire Cricket Club president Richard Plant.

Staffordshire's legendary cricketer Sydney Barnes watching a Minor Counties match in 1966, the year before he died at the age of 94. In his prime before the 1914-18 war he was described as the best bowler in the world. Barnes played in 27 Test matches for England and performed record-breaking feats against Australia and South Africa. Uniquely, he played for England while he was club professional with Porthill Park in the North Staffs League. Barnes played his last match for Staffordshire when he was 62 and in 1940, at the age of 67, he turned out for Stone as an amateur. He bowled his last over in competitive cricket at the age of 80 in a testimonial match at Stafford. In his working life Barnes was a calligraphist in Staffordshire County Council's legal department.

A welcome guest at a cricket dinner in 1963 was the
ex-England and Lancashire wicket keeper George
Duckworth, pictured here with his hosts. On the extreme
left is Arthur Hodson, president and long-time official
of the North Staffordshire and District League. On the
right of the group is Doug Scholfield, league secretary,
and behind him Ken Higgs, the former Sandyford player
who joined Lancashire and won several England caps.
Higgs was the first graduate from the Kidsgrove Junior
League to play in first-class county cricket.

A crowd of 3,000 saw the North Staffs and South Cheshire League team regain the Rothman Trophy after their victory in the final of the competition at Chell in 1969. They beat the Northern League by 39 runs to win the inter-league prize for the second time in four years. The winners are pictured with the umpires. The team was: Arthur Sutton (Newcastle and Hartshill), Nasim-ul-Ghani (Longton), Barry Coates (Leek), Vic Babb (Porthill), Geoff Hardstaff (Newcastle and Hartshill), Gerry Sobers (Norton), Brian Jackson (Knypersley), Bill Taylor (Leek), Peter Howell (Bignall End), Les Lowe (Knypersley) and David Brock (Newcastle and Hartshill).

Throughout the 1960s Bernard Hollowood was a leading figure in British journalism as editor of the satirical magazine Punch. A man of incisive wit, he took over from Malcolm Muggeridge after many years as a contributor, both as a writer and a cartoonist. He was also an authority on pottery design. In the 1930s he was captain of Burslem Cricket Club's championship-winning side, playing alongside his two brothers. Hollowood, who died in 1981, was an old boy of Hanley High School.

Former England cricketer Jack Ikin, centre, welcomes his old Lancashire colleague, Jack Dyson, at Bignall End in 1965, while Vince Lindo looks on. During his fine Test career all-rounder Ikin established an international reputation for his brilliant fielding. He played for Bignall End as a boy and later returned to his home club, also taking over the captaincy of Staffordshire. When Vince Lindo arrived in Britain in 1962 he might have graduated into first-class county cricket as a fast bowler with Nottinghamshire. But he opted to stick to North Staffordshire league cricket and was still hitting centuries for Hanford when he was past 60.

Norton professional Garfield Sobers draws out the first names for a single-wicket competition at the club in 1967. It was played for the Frank Worrell memorial trophy, presented by club chairman Tom Talbot, who is holding the silver cup. Other Norton officials in the picture are Eric Glaze, Jim Johnson and Len Parton, the latter also wellknown as Stoke City's groundsman. On the right are Norton captain Jim Flannery and Jesse Hall, captain of visiting team Sneyd.

In 1960 Great Chell cricket club embarked on a programme of ground improvements with the opening of this electronically-operated scoreboard. It was followed by a new stand seating 750 people and a replacement pavilion. In the centre of the picture is Dennis Haynes, president of the North Staffs and District Cricket League. To the right are Len Barber, club chairman, and Doug Scholfield, financial secretary. In 1963 Great Chell were among clubs who broke away to form a North Staffs and South Cheshire League. Subsequently, the club's fortunes faded dramatically and it is no longer in existence.

Formed out of a sunken garden, Clough Hall bowling club at Kidsgrove became known as the bowling green in the hole. It was launched in 1906 as a private club and over the years has maintained an average membership of around 70. In 1945 the club acquired a wooden building used as a grocery shop and converted it into a pavilion. The club's trophies have included the F S Jones Cup, the Stubbs Cup and, in 2002, the Sentinel Cup. Clough Hall stalwarts Arthur Brewood (left) and Bill Sandham are seen in play in the 1960s, watched by fellow members.

No-one knew more about the life and times of Izaak Walton, Staffordshire's "father of anglers", than the man who looked after his cottage for 25 years. Jim Popple, curator and caretaker, welcomed visitors from all over the world to Walton's little museum at Shallowford, near Eccleshall. Jim could come up with the text from practically any page of Walton's monumental work The Compleat Angler. He is pictured with the Mayor of Stafford, Coun S H Robinson, in 1966 when the trusteeship of the cottage was vested in Stafford Corporation.

Star sprinter Dorothy Window (nee Hindmarsh) winning a race by a comfortable margin at Cobridge Stadium in 1962. Dorothy was one of a crop of women athletes with the City of Stoke AC who rose to international level in the late 1950s. She was the first woman from North Staffordshire to compete in the European Games, reaching the semi-finals of the 80 metres hurdles in Belgrade in 1962.

This quartet of female runners were Stoke-on-Trent's leading ladies in 1960. They were the first athletics team from the Potteries to win a senior national trophy, capturing the women's national sprint relay title at White City. It was also the first time the event had been won by a team from outside London. The four runners (left to right) are Ann Pover, Rosemary Wilshaw, Kathleen Degg and Dorothy Hindmarsh. Holding the trophy is Leonard Ward, Stoke-on-Trent athletics advisor and coach to the City of Stoke Athletic Club. The team celebrated their victory with dinner at the Dorchester Hotel.

Veteran athlete Dai Benson, aged 60, receives his final prize for running from Lady Mayoress Mrs Dale at the 1960 Michelin Sports. This was North Staffordshire's biggest outdoor sporting of the year outside football and temporary stands were erected to accommodate crowds of up to 5,000 spectators at the tyre company's sports ground in Campbell Road, Stoke. High-class athletes and cyclists from all over the Midlands took part. The annual event later moved to a new Michelin sports ground at Trent Vale.

With their distinctive five-star colours, Stoke Potters were still drawing the crowds to the Sun Street Stadium, Hanley, in 1962. In this picture Stoke promoter Reg Fearman is seen with three local riders who took part in a first round meeting in the world championship. From the left, the trio are Peter Jarman, Pete Adams and Ken Adams. Speedway finished at Sun Street in 1963 after being staged for three seasons. Meetings had previously been held there in the 1940s and early 1950s, attracting crowds of up to 20,000.

Start of the first race at the Shelton cycle speedway track after its official opening on October 15, 1967, before a crowd of 250 people. The purpose-built circuit was located close to the site of Stoke Speedway stadium. Previously, riders had operated on home-made tracks. Teams competing in a local league at that time included Shelton Tigers, Bucknall Saints, Bradwell Bulldogs and Heron Cross Hammers.

Stoke Potters had two post-war spells at the Hanley Stadium before speedway was wound up at Sun Street in 1963. This picture was taken at the first bend in 1962, with two Stoke riders in the lead. In the first speedway era from 1946-53, the meetings at Sun Street attracted crowds of up to 20,000.

One of the last pictures to be taken of Stoke Potters speedway riders before the Sun Street Stadium closed in 1963. Seated on the bike is skipper Ken Adams and others in the picture include Ray Harris, Colin Pratt, Pete Jarman, Ron Sharp and Eric Hockaday. The promoter and former rider Reg Fearman is on the right.

Stoke Speedway supporters pictured with new rider Peter Jarman at the old Hanley Stadium in 1960. This second spell of speedway at Sun Street was short-lived, as racing finished in 1963. Jarman later returned to the area in 1978 to become team manager of Stoke Potters at their new home at Loomer Road, Chesterton.

Les West and Bernadette Swinnerton, who put their native Stoke-on-Trent on the international cycling map in the 1960s. As an amateur, West won the Tour of Britain Milk Race in both 1965 and 1967 and finished second in the world road race championship in 1966. He competed in the Mexico Olympics in 1968 before turning professional. Bernadette won the British women's sprint title in 1968 when she was only 17 and the half-mile grass track championship. She was silver medallist in the road race at the world championships in Rome and was also runner-up in the British road race for women.

With Etruria Hall in the background, Shelton steelworkers take on Biddulph Town in a football match in 1961. The sports ground was situated in a prominent position in front of the works and both football and cricket matches were clearly visible to passers-by on Etruria Road. The land was reclaimed by filling in a pool, although water has since returned to this spot with the construction of a canalside marina.

Ray Reardon watches his young opponent David Taylor, of Manchester, in a professional match at Wolstanton Mine Welfare Club, Smallthorne, in 1969. Reardon came to the Potteries as a miner in 1955 and later spent eight years in the police force, winning the British police snooker championship four times before turning professional. He won the first of his six world titles in 1970.

Even in an exhibition game, snooker ace Ray Reardon displays the concentration which brought him the world professional snooker title on six occasions. He is seen in action here in 1969 at Tunstall British Legion Club. Watching are Ray Shaw, Ken Birk, Tom Holland and George Dunn. At the time the former Hanley policeman was preparing for his semi-final match with Fred Davis in the world championship. He was Stoke-on-Trent's first world champion in any sport.

Sir Stanley Matthews and Jackie Mudie pose beneath the official entrance to Vale Park in July 1965 after the Stoke City legend took over as the new manager of Port Vale. Matthews and Mudie had played together at both Blackpool and Stoke. But Sir Stanley's spell at Vale Park ended abruptly when Vale were briefly expelled from the Football League in 1968 for breaking the rules over payments.

It was an occasion never to be forgotten when Sir Stanley Matthews played in his farewell match at the Victoria Ground on April 28, 1965. Famous players from many countries turned out to pay tribute to the soccer legend. In this line-up the player nearest the camera is a youthful Jimmy Greaves (then of Spurs), followed by Bryan Douglas (Blackburn Rovers), Alan Gilzean (Spurs), Johnny Haynes (Fulham), Jim Baxter (Rangers), Cliff Jones (Spurs), Ron Flowers (Wolves), Tony Waiters (Blackpool) and George Cohen (Fulham). Others who played included Ferenc Puskas (Hungary), Alfredo di Stefano (Spain) and Lev Yashin (Russia).

The glittering career of Stanley Matthews reached a fitting climax in 1965 when the Wizard of Dribble became the first professional footballer to receive a knighthood. Sir Stan, second left, is pictured outside Buckingham Palace with his wife Betty, son Stanley junior, daughter Jean Gough and her husband Bobby. On the extreme left is the Sentinel's Stoke City reporter, Norman Gosling, who attended the ceremony as a close friend.

A dramatic moment as Dennis Viollet beats the goalkeeper to score Stoke City's first goal against Real Madrid at the Victoria Ground on April 24, 1963. The match, watched by a crowd of 45,000, was staged to mark Stoke's centenary. It ended in a 2-2 draw. In the background is the old directors' box. The Boothen Stand was then unfinished and some spectators sat in the open air.

A view from the press box at Stoke City's old Victoria Ground, taken during the Stan Matthews farewell match in April 1965. The comedian Charlie Chester, Stan's old friend, entertained the crowd at the microphone set up in front of the stand. The linesman on the right was Roy Capey, one of North Staffordshire's handful of referees who graduated to the Football League.

Admiring fans carried Stoke City striker Dennis Viollet off the field after his final appearance at the Victoria Ground in 1967 in his own testimonial match. Viollet, a former "Busby Babe" with Manchester United and survivor of the Munich air crash, became an idol of the crowd during his five-year career with Stoke. He scored 66 goals in just over 200 games. Later, he managed Linfield and Crewe Alexandra before emigrating to America. After his death, Viollet's ashes were scattered over the Britannia Stadium, Stoke's present home ground, even though he never played there.

Ferenc Puskas, one of Hungary's "Magical Magyars" of the 1950s, scores with a perfect penalty kick for Real Madrid to make the score 2-2 in Stoke City's centenary match in 1963. The respective captains were Stanley Matthews and Alfredo di Stefano. At a banquet afterwards, the Real Madrid party said they had never been treated so well anywhere else in the world.

Stoke City's full complement of players pictured at the Victoria Ground at the start of the 1962-63 promotion season, with manager Tony Waddington seated centre. Stan Matthews, second left in the second row, had rejoined the club in 1961 and was then 47. Mr Waddington was the most succesful manager in Stoke's history.

It looks as if this flock of sheep had just wandered onto Stoke City's old Victoria Ground in 1963. But they were herded onto the pitch with the full approval of the club as a novel means of keeping the grass down in summer. The picture showed the progress being made on the new Boothen Stand, which replaced a much inferior structure dating back to the 1900s. However, the final stage of the modern stand still remained uncompleted when the new football season began.

There were jubilant scenes at the Victoria Ground in 1963 when Stoke City clinched promotion and the Division II championship by beating Luton Town 2-0 in their final home game. Thousands of fans invaded the pitch to salute the Stoke players, who climbed up into the stand. Stan Matthews is seen waving to the crowd, with Stoke's skipper Eddie Stuart and Eric Skeels on the left. Matthews scored Stoke's second goal to seal an historic victory.

Although Stan Matthews never won a Sentinel Cup medal, he knew how much they are treasured by former junior footballers. At the annual dinner of the Sentinel football competitions in 1964, he recalled that his old manager at Blackpool, Joe Smith, had said he would never part with the Sentinel Cup medal he won with Chesterton PSA in 1908. Principal guests at the dinner were (seated, left to right): Ted Adams (chairman), Richard Austen (president and Sentinel general manager), Stan Matthews, John Tupholme (Editor of the Sentinel), life member Fred Wright and Port Vale director Tom Talbot.

Stoke City players mob Stanley Matthews after he had scored Stoke's second goal against Luton Town in 1963. The 2-0 victory at the Victoria Ground clinched the Second Division championship and promotion to the top flight. Matthews had returned to Stoke 18 months earlier at the age of 46.

Port Vale began the 1960-61 season in thre Third Division with a first-team squad of 22 players and Manager Norman Low in his third year with the club. A year earlier, Vale had become the first champions of the new Fourth Division. In the picture the players are as follows:- Top row, left to right: Selwyn Whalley, Dennis Fidler, Ted Calland, Peter Ford, Harry Poole, Graham Barnett; second row: Roy Gater, Peter Hall, John Poole, Ken Hancock, Roy Sproson, Terry Lowe; third row: Terry Miles, Cliff Portwood, Norman Low (manager), Albert Leake, John Archer, David Raine; bottom row: Noel Kinsey, Stan Steele, Barry Hancock, Colin Davies, Brian Jackson.

Port Vale might not have reached the cup final, but they did win a cup in 1962. It was the Giant Killer Cup, awarded by a national newspaper for the best performance by a club from the lower leagues in the FA Cup. Vale were the sixth club to win it, although the prize was discontinued soon afterwards. Vale captain John Nicholson is seen holding the trophy aloft.

# Transport & Emergency Services

After centuries of isolation, North Staffordshire came much nearer to the outside world in the 1960s. Rail passengers said goodbye to the Potteries Loop Line and the old steam railways and entered a new era of high-speed travel. Electric trains halved the journey time to London. On the road drivers went into top gear with the opening of the M6 motorway. It was also a time of change for the vital services. In 1968 Stoke-on-Trent lost its independent police force, which amalgamated with Staffordshire Police. And the city ambulance service moved from its old depot in Campbell Road, Stoke, to new headquarters at Harpfields, close to the hospitals.

Burslem Station on the old Potteries Loop Line in 1962, viewed from Hamil Road railway bridge. A short freight train is leaving the station on the north-bound line. The station's unusually large booking hall is in the background on the right, with the tall buildings of Burslem Baths on the left. Opened in 1873, the station closed in the 1960s a few years short of its centenary. The novelist Arnold Bennett was among its early passengers. Picture by Geoff Sutton.

An occasional puff of steam was the only indication that a little railway station lay beneath the busy A34 road just north of Newcastle. Most people didn't know that Liverpool Road Halt was there. It was used mainly by workers at the nearby Enderley Mills, or by day trippers heading for the races at Mucklestone and Woore. The station was opened in the early 1900s by the old North Staffordshire Railway in an attempt to compete with the trams for short-run passengers. The picture, from the collection of transport historian Basil Jeuda, was taken in the early 1960s.

What was happening here? In 1960 engineers from the MEB laid an "electric blanket" of wiring under the road surface on the steepest part of Friars Street. The objective was to keep it clear of ice and snow in winter. At the time the experiment was the first of its kind in the Midlands.

One of the last passenger trains to stop at Market Drayton railway station before it closed to passengers services in September 1963. The station, on the Crewe to Wellington line for nearly a century, was busy during the 1939-45 war because of the close proximity of several RAF airfields in North Shropshire. In the 1950s the stationmaster was a man named Hemmings who was also an all-in wrestler.

Railway lines curve through sidings off Etruria Road towards Hanley Station in this unusual view of the Potteries Loop Line taken shortly before passenger trains ended in the mid-1960s. Prominent in the background are the Grand Hotel and the old Trinity telephone exchange. The site of the goods yard on the right is now a carpark.

The last steam locomotive hissed out of the Stoke Sheds on August 10, 1967, ending a railway era which began well over a century earlier. Situated behind a row of cottages off City Road, Fenton, the two sheds were built by the North Staffordshire Railway, close to the Knotty's landmark Roundhouse. They could accommodate up to 80 locos, which were largely employed on freight haulage carrying coal, sand and clay. The picture shows a British Rail Standard type 2-6-0 engine moving out of the empty sheds. On the extreme right is shedmaster Ralph Blunt. With him are fireman Alan Jenkinson, driver Len Simpson and boilersmiths Jack Oldfield and Sydney Smith.

If there was a heavy lifting job to be done at the old Shelton Steelworks, Dubsey could usually handle it. The specialist tank engine with a built-in crane did yeoman service at the works for more than 70 years after arriving at Shelton in 1901 from the makers, Dubs and Co of Glasgow. In 1973 Dubsey was purchased by the East Somerset Railway, but was brought back to North Staffordshire in 1998. Steam enthusiast Dave Scragg has restored this unique locomotive at the Foxfield Steam Railway, Blythe Bridge.

Passenger services on the Potteries Loop Line passed into history in 1965 when this special train carrying rail enthusiasts made the final run over the eight-mile stretch from Kidsgrove to Etruria. The picture was taken by former railwayman Geoff Sutton as the locomotive came over the summit near his home at Newchapel. Hired by Manchester University Railway Society, the train carried the name-board The Staffordshire Potter. The Loop Line, often mentioned in novels by Arnold Bennett, was part of Potteries life for nearly a century.

Thousands of passengers used Hanley Station in the first half of the 20th century when the Potteries Loop Line still played a major role in public transport. Early morning trains called on the way to Manchester and in the late evening the station was packed with people going home from theatres and cinemas. The picture shows the silent platforms in 1963 shortly before passenger trains were withdrawn from the line. In the Second World War the station was hit by incendiary bombs during an air raid in 1941.

Newcastle's railway station was only on a branch line from Stoke to Market Drayton, yet it welcomed more royal trains than any other station of its size in the Midlands. This was mainly because Princess Margaret often travelled to Newcastle by train during her long association with Keele University. Other royal visitors, including Queen Elizabeth II, have stepped down onto the short platform. The station was situated in a cutting opposite the Borough Arms Hotel. At one end, trains entered the station almost straight out of a two-part tunnel which passed under Basford. After the station closed in 1965 the cutting was filled in to form a public walkway.

This old steam locomotive, one of the last to be made by the North Staffordshire Railway (The Knotty), came back to its roots in Stoke in 1960. It is seen in display in a siding just outside Stoke Station in an exhibition featuring several historic engines, staged as part of Stoke-on-Trent's golden jubilee celebrations. The L-class locomotive, made in 1923, was specially repainted and restored to its original deep-red Knotty livery. In 1937 it was sold for shunting work at a colliery near Manchester and loaned for the centenary event. However, it is now back home permanently at the Cheddleton headquarters of the Churnet Valley Railway.

A team of railwaymen polished this LMS locomotive to perfection when it was hired by Lewis's Store in Hanley to haul the Santa Claus train into Stoke Station. Father Christmas was picked up by a signal box and after a short journey the train arrived at Platform One. If the weather was fine, Santa and his attendants continued the journey to Hanley in a horse-drawn carriage. The picture was taken in 1960 by James Amison, a loco driver from Longton who worked on the Santa Special.

Stoke-on-Trent City Reconstruction Officer Jim Plant pictured in 1962 with models of the proposed Bennett Precinct at Longton on the site of the old bus station. The models went on public display in Longton Town Hall. The first stage of the scheme was completed in 1965. It was named after council leader Sir Albert Bennett, a leading figure in the post-war redevelopment of the city. The shopping precinct was only the second to be built in the country, following the first one at Coventry.

Longton's original bus station had the distinction of being the first one to be laid out in North Staffordshire. Indeed, when this picture was taken in 1963 it was still the only purpose-built bus station. However, the location was unattractive, with derelict pottery premises close by. On the far side is the PMT snack bar and the Bull's Head pub. The whole area was cleared to make way for the Bennett shopping precinct. A covered bus station with a bowling alley was built nearby at Commerce Street. The bowling alley was later turned into Jollees night club.

Port Vale's former home, the Old Recreation Ground in Hanley, was still recognisable in 1961 long after the pitch had been turned into Stoke-on-Trent's first paying carpark. At that time the St John's Church was still functioning, as was the even taller Hanley Tabernacle on the left, though these extensive church premises in Town Road were already earmarked for demolition. The old ground is now covered by the Potteries shopping centre carpark.

Poole's Buses, a family firm started at Alsagers Bank in 1925, survived much longer than many other small bus operators. At their peak, Poole's had a fleet of 15 maroon and ivory painted vehicles, although their services were concentrated on a small area around Newcastle. Their helpful crews had a reputation for stopping almost anywhere to pick up passengers. The picture shows a Poole's bus at Newcastle bus station in 1960.

Before the opening of the M6 motorway through North Staffordshire in 1963, pedestrians in Newcastle had to contend with an endless procession of traffic passing through the town in both directions. This 1961 picture illustrates the hazards of crossing the High Street, then part of the A34 trunk road. A little further down the road, south-bound vehicles passed within a few feet of busy stalls on the open-air market.

Piccadilly Circus and Trafalgar Square were among the regular stopping-places for these former London Transport buses before they arrived in Hanley around 1960. They were purchased by Beckett's, a bus company which ran services from Ash Bank into Hanley for many years until the company was taken over by PMT in 1963. The London buses remained on the road for some time afterwards. The pair in the picture are seen outside the old Essoldo Cinema, Hanley, in 1961.

Tom Byatt was a dealer in British cars like Morris, Austin, Jaguar, Rover and Triumph from a garage with an art deco frontage at Victoria Road, Fenton. It opened in 1936 and in post-war years became one of the best-known garages and car showrooms in North Staffordshire when run by the founder's son, Tom Byatt junior. The Byatt motor trading empire eventually extended to five companies. The picture was taken in 1960 in one of the hangar-like workshops. The business finished in the 1980s and the site is now occupied by retail stores.

Stoke-on-Trent Special Constabulary Band, pictured here in 1966, was formed out of a wartime Home Guard band in the 1940s. All the band members became special constables and carried on under the new title. They practised on Sunday mornings in the assembly hall at Hanley Police Station. One of the conductors had previously played with the famous Fodens Motorworks Band. Seated behind the big drum is the late Chief Constable of Stoke-on-Trent, William Watson. The city force merged with Staffordshire county police two years later.

A fleet of Bedford ambulances lined up in 1966 at the old city depot off Campbell Road, Stoke, two years before the base was moved to Harpfields. When the council-run operation was first launched in 1948 it covered the whole city with just six vehicles. They were garaged in a group of Nissen huts left over from the war. Early crews had little formal training and had to make do with a box of bandages and a few splints.

Stoke-on-Trent detectives and their wives were in party mood when this picture was taken at a New Year's Eve Police Ball at the Victoria Hall, Hanley, in the early 1960s. In the foreground is Detective Superintendent Harry Steele, who later became assistant chief constable in the old city force. The police ball was the only dance of the year held at the Victoria Hall.

Many of these faces were well known to criminals in the Potteries in the 1960s. It was the final get-together of senior police officers in the old Stoke-on-Trent city force before amalgamation with Staffordshire county police in 1968. Seated are Assistant Chief Constable Harry Steele, Lord Mayor Edwin Holloway, Chief Constable William Watson and Joe Hulme, chairman of the city watch committee.

Sergeant Ronald Biggs pictured at Newcastle in 1963 before giving a talk on road
safety. He was welcomed by Newcastle Mayor Sydney Whalley, along with police
chiefs Ray Hazell and Albert Howard and Newcastle's road safety organiser Wallace
Anderson (on right). Two years later Sgt Biggs was among the first policemen on the
scene at a crash on the M6 at Hanchurch in which four people were killed. He was
chosen to attend an emergency meeting at the Ministry of Transport at which a ruling
was made to set a speed limit of 70mph, as a direct result of the Hanchurch crash. Sgt
Biggs finished his police career as a chief superintendent.

Stoke Police Station was open 24 hours a day during
the whole of its 80 years in the service of law and order.
The chief inspector in charge actually lived in part of
the solid-looking Victorian building in Copeland Street,
Stoke. The chief's home, with a separate entrance, can
be seen on the extreme right of this 1968 picture. For
many years the Lord Mayor's chain of office was taken
to the police station for safe keeping every night. The
building was one of many demolished in the early 1970s
to make way for the construction of the A500 road
through Stoke.